Mom, remember when you said
if I ever,
you know,
thought about,
well,
like having sex with someone
or something like that I shouldn't be afraid
to, you know, talk to you about,
you know,
like birth control and stuff.
I mean, you wouldn't freak or anything.
So, I was just wondering…
Uh, Mom, are you listening to me?

      You bet.

Susan Fulop Kepner
1987

Other works by Susan Fulop Kepner

Six Slums in Bangkok
A Child of the Northeast (Translator/editor)
Letters From Thailand (Translator/editor)

Somebody's Mother

SUSAN FULOP KEPNER

illustrated by MARTHA WESTON

Strawberry Hill Press

Strawberry Hill Press
2594 15th Avenue
San Francisco, California 94127

Illustrations, layout, design and cover by Martha Weston

Typeset by Cragmont Publications, Oakland, California

Printed by Edwards Brothers, Inc., Lillington, North Carolina

Manufactured in the United States of America

An earlier version of "I Like You Better Now" appeared in *McCall's*, October, 1986

Library of Congress Cataloging–in–Publication Data

Kepner, Susan Fulop, 1941–
    Somebody's mother.

    1. Adolescence—Anecdotes, facetia, satire, etc.
2. Mother and child—Anecdotes, facetia, satire, etc.
I. Weston, Martha.   II. Title.
PN6231.A26K47   1987   811'.54   87–18003
ISBN 0–89407–088–6 (pbk.)

This is for

Tom and Nick, Julie and Annie

Table of Contents

Two Boys, Two Girls

Junior High School

High School

Life After High School

TWO BOYS, TWO GIRLS

When we were in high school, Eleanor,
you used to talk about
how you were going to have
two boys and two girls,
and that way everybody would have
a big sister to talk to,
and a big brother to bring home guys,
and a little sister to read stories to.
Even then, I knew there was
a flaw in the logic somewhere, and now I know
that there were quite a few.
I want you to know
how the plan turned out, Eleanor,
since you ended up with one kid and joint custody,
and I ended up with two boys and two girls.

What it meant
was that all of them had at least one sibling
they hated at first sight in its receiving blanket
and forever after,
and one who was smarter
and brought it up frequently,
and one who could be counted on
to embarrass everyone to death
on all special occasions,
and one who was
extremely popular and pretended not to be related.

What it meant
was that I started out
with four babies who were adorable,
and that slowly and surely
they turned into four teenagers
who were not.

Junior High School

SLUGS

I did *not* say that your marinated eggplant tasted
like cut–up slugs. I said it
looked like cut–up slugs
and in my mouth
it sort of *felt* like
what I would imagine
cut–up slugs
would feel like.

Oh Jeez, a person can't
say anything around here
without somebody getting all hyper.
It's just that slugs have these
shiny little purple skins and—
All right! All right!
I won't say another word.

Rob, just tell me the truth,
not to be on my side or anything.
Am I crazy or does this eggplant
look like cut–up slugs? Not *taste* like them,
I am not talking about taste,
but wouldn't you admit that they look like them?

See, Mom, I am not crazy. Even Rob—

All right! All right! I'll stop!
Look, I'm stopping!
I will say nothing.
Nothing at all.
We will have it just the way you want it.
We will sit here together
at our family dinner table
and not talk.

SWEETBREADS

My friend Christie's father
took them out to dinner
to this fancy place where you get, like,
breadsticks and water and everything,
and her brother Kevin ordered this stuff called sweetbreads
because everything else on the menu looked gross
and he thought they'd bring him a Danish or something
but they brought him this seriously bad stuff,
sort of like liver but even worse.
He could hardly believe it.
I mean, he said it looked like mushrooms that have been
in the refrigerator for about a month.

Oh, finally his dad ate it.

And then when they got home
Kevin put some Beefaroni in the microwave
because he was practically starving
and his dad started yelling at him.

Who knows?
His dad always gets mad like that
about nothing.

GROSS

Cottage cheese is gross
and lamb is gross. Skim milk
is gross ultimate.

     Don't you know any other word?

Oh, look at that girl—
Her hair is too gross. Those little
gross bangs and everything.

     Don't they teach you any adjectives in school?

A girl in my class
has these gross earrings.
Each one is a little tooth
and she has a little toothbrush necklace
that matches and a bracelet
that looks like braces.
Isn't that gross?

     Now that is gross.

TOTALLY BORED

There must be something you can do.
If you're really desperate
you and Jennifer can always
go down to the meat department at the Safeway
and gross yourselves out
looking at the tongues and brains.

So what if you did it yesterday?
Who knows?
Maybe they got pig's feet in today.

CREAMED TUNA

Oh, *ick*—
What is that you're making?

Creamed tuna.

Hey, Mom.
Wanna know what it looks like?

No.

FRIED EGGS

Oh, Mom, I almost forgot,
tomorrow it's my turn
in our cooking project.
How many fried eggs should I take for thirty kids?

But you don't understand—it's my *assignment*!
I *have* to!
Everybody has to take a turn.
What?
Oh, they brought different stuff.
Felicia brought this disgusting peanut butter health candy
and a boy said it looked like dog doo and she cried.
Well, it did.

I thought I could take the eggs
in a big Zip–loc bag or something.

Do you think they'll stay warm?

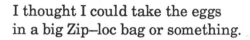

WHAT SHE'S INTO

Four years ago, she says,
I was into stickers.
Three years ago,
I was into Barbie and Jem.
I can hardly believe it.
I mean, it seems like a hundred years ago.
It seems like I was a baby then.

Last year I was into clothes
and Teddy bears.
This year I'm still into clothes
and sort of into Teddy bears
but I'm also into earrings
and boys.
Last year all the boys were nasty,
but this year some of them are sort of nice.

What year do you get
"into" studying?

Mom, I don't think you understand.
You don't get "into"
stuff you have to do.

Oh, I don't know.
Plenty of people are "into"
their jobs
even though they have to do them.

Yeah, right. They're grownups.

Yes, but do you get my point?

Sure. When you're a grownup
you figure out how to like
stuff you actually hate.

Come on. Remember when you were little
and you hated cottage cheese,
but then you got to like it?

That was Rob, Mom. I hated it then,
I hate it now,
and I will hate it forever.

I think this conversation has peaked.

Really.

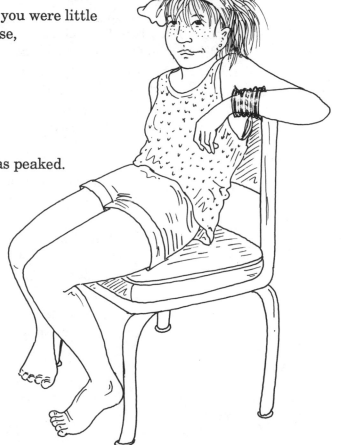

SCHOOL PICTURES

Tomorrow we get our eighth grade picture taken.
I always do something
to make myself look
ridiculous.

> That's not true.
> All your school pictures are very nice.

Oh come on, Mom. In my seventh grade picture
I smiled too big
and all you could see
was a hundred braces
and in my sixth grade picture
one of my braids stuck out
like I was Pippi Longstocking or something
and in my fifth grade picture
you could see my tongue
and in my fourth grade picture
I wore that dumb Strawberry Shortcake blouse.

> Now wait a minute.
> You insisted on wearing
> your Strawberry Shortcake blouse.

Well, you shouldn't have let me.

> Sorry, love, but nobody
> gets to blame me later
> for the results
> of the arguments I lost.

PIERCED EARS

I don't care
if Stephanie's mother
let her get her ears triple pierced.
Stephanie can look like she's wearing
two colanders on her head for all I care.

Stephanie can have
her nose pierced for all I care.

You're *kidding*...

GEEKS

Dad just told me something
I have to ask you about.

      Shoot.

This is really embarrassing.
He said that when he was in junior high
he was one of the geeks.

      Really?

I mean, your own father,
a geek?
I wonder if he understands, Mom,
what it means
to be a geek.

      Oh, I think he understands.

And then he said he's grateful
Sesame Street didn't start
until he was grown up,
whatever that means.
Why are you laughing?

Haven't you ever seen
that eighth grade picture of your Dad?

Yeah...
Oh my God,
Kermit.

Well, my eighth grade picture
didn't win any prizes either.

I know. You sort of looked like
Peppermint Patty. I don't want to
hurt your feelings or anything,
but it is amazing to me
that two people like you and Dad
could have had four kids like us.

Believe me, Margaret, it is not half
as amazing to you
as it is to us.

CLASS OF 1962

THE GENTLE ART OF CONVERSATION

Phone Call One

So then Melanie goes, "Ri–i–i–ght,"
and I'm like, oh my God.
And then Alexis says,
"Melanie, you can't be serious,"
and she goes,
"Su–u–u–re, Margaret,"
and I'm like, oh my God.
He is so *buff*...
I don't know if he likes me.
Do you think he likes me?
You can't be serious.

Phone Call Two

So then Tracy goes, "Are you serious?"
and I go, "Ri–i–i–ght,"
and Melanie is like, oh my God.
And Monica says,
"Margaret, you can't be serious,"
and I go,
"Su–u–u–re, Monica,"
and she's like, oh my God.
She doesn't know if he likes her.
Do you think he likes her?
You can't be serious.

Epilogue

This is why I need my own phone, Mom,
because I really hate it when
I'm having a private conversation
and there are people walking around here
listening to everything I say.

You can't be serious.

COLLECTIONS

I am up to here with
Gummi Worms and Gummi anything and
Teddy bears and Super–Heroes and Wonder–People
and dolls with creepy little voices
and bodily functions.

It is time to start giving
some of this stuff away, and I say,
the Care Bears go first.

To tell you the truth,
I can still remember when I was thirteen
and my mom finally made me give away
my Hopalong Cassidy plastic swim–ring with
the horse's head and black plastic reins,
and my Howdy Doody records,
and my Dale Rogers boots,
and even my Kukla, Fran and Ollie hand puppets.
I was really mad.

Now, if I had all that stuff today,
It would be worth something.
Thank God I hid my Howdy Doody records from her.

      Mom, if you could keep Howdy Doody records,
      why can't I keep Papa Smurf?

Don't be ridiculous, Margaret.
Howdy Doody is a *legend*.

High School

HOW CAN YOU LIVE LIKE THIS?

So this mother pig
waddles across the sty
to where a young pig
is curled up in one corner
surrounded by all kinds of garbage.

Old bags of stale corn chips,
candy bars melted to their wrappers,
Pepsi cans with an inch left
in the bottom, and
he doesn't even notice,
he just lies there, chewing on pizza scraps
and thinking about things.

And the mother pig says,
"How can you live like this?
It looks like a teen–ager's bedroom."

SOMEBODY'S MOTHER

You will never believe this
because it is too weird but
yesterday Wendy saw you walking out of
Hudson's Pharmacy and she thought you were a kid,
can you believe it?

You can?

Anyway, yeah, she really thought you were a kid
so she wondered who you were, like,
maybe you just moved here or something.

What?
Oh, you were wearing jeans
and running shoes I guess, not your
usual mother clothes.

Mother clothes? You know, those ironed blouses,
the fish–head shoes,
the usual.
I said, "Get serious Wendy,
I know she's short but
didn't you look at her face or anything?
Or the gray hair?"

She said she didn't have her contacts in
so she had to get real close and then
it was too weird, because, you know,
when she got up close,
it wasn't anybody.

Just somebody's mother.

POLITICS

She and the best friend,
giggling in the back seat.
If only she had her license
but she doesn't have her license
and so I drive
from mall to mall to mall,
cherishing the even,
rational national voice
of National Public Radio turned down low,
just for me,
while what Lacey said to Tracy about Stacey
fills the rest of the car like an airbag.

Carlos Fuentes is reading a poem about El Salvador
in the front seat.
The girls are reading Jennifer's letter about Richard
in the back seat.
MacNeil and Lehrer are concerned about
Daniel Ortega and Mikhail Gorbachev and Howard Baker
in the front seat.
The girls are concerned about
Michael and Danny and Martin
and Peter and Alex and Roger
in the back seat.

Later, a stranger asks,
"What are you girls interested in?"
"Oh, politics and stuff," one says.
"Yeah," the other adds.

SEX OR SOMETHING LIKE THAT

Mom, I was just thinking about the time
when I was, like, ten or something and you
told me all about periods
and the facts of life and stuff.
Remember?

       You bet.

Well, that reminded me of
when I was, like, thirteen
and Phyllis in my class got pregnant
and had a kid.

       And named him U2 Yovanovich?

Yeah. At first
she was gonna name him Bon Jovi,
but she didn't think it went with Yovanovich.
God, she was dumb.
You remember that?

       You bet.

Anyway, you said
if I ever,
you know,
thought about,
well,
like having sex with someone
or something like that
I shouldn't be afraid
to, you know, talk to you about,
you know,
like birth control and stuff.
I mean, you wouldn't freak or anything.
So, I was just wondering...
Uh, Mom, are you listening to me?

       You bet.

I NEVER TALKED TO MY MOTHER
THE WAY YOU TALK TO ME

I never talked to my mother
the way you talk to me.
I wouldn't have dared.
Are you kidding?
If I ever talked to my mother
the way you talk to me,
well, I wouldn't have dreamed
of talking to her
the way you talk to me.

Oddly enough,
my mother once told me
that she never talked to her mother
the way I talked to her.
Never.

And it may be that her mother
never talked to *her* mother
the way my mother talked to,
uh, to my grandmother,
that is,
your great–grandmother,
who may,
for all we know,
never have talked to her mother at all.
Out of respect.

SENIORS VISIT NATION'S CAPITAL

Mom, could you just try to have an open mind?
At least look at the brochure.
It's the only chance I'll ever have
to spend a week in Washington
with congressmen and senators
and going to the Supreme Court and stuff.
You're always saying that I
have no interest in current events
and now I have this opportunity
to spend an entire week
learning exactly how the Government works
and practically all my friends are going
and all you can ask
is what it costs.

      How true.

Look, when I go to college
I might even major in political science
as a direct result of this trip
but do you think of that?
Oh, no. You ask, **How much?**

       Listen, Rob, if you want to know
       the truth, I'll tell you:
       It sounds like party–time to me
       and this brochure has
       everything but price.

All right. Fifty bucks by Friday
and the other seven hundred in a month.
Oh God, here comes the *look*.
Oh, this is *so* like you.
I *knew* you'd be this way.

       Seven hundred fifty bucks?

But that's including everything!

       Seven hundred fifty *bucks*?

Well, so much for a Government career.

THE BEHAVIOR NOT THE PERSON

I know that you are a fine and sensitive
caring and perceptive and wonderful *person*
way, way down deep,
where we cannot see it.
And I know that it is not you
that is, not you as a *person*,
but your *behavior*
which at this moment
I find provocative, rude, and,
let's face it, despicable.
And while I would not
for the world
dream of doing anything
or saying anything
that could have a negative effect
on your self–esteem
(God forbid),
in the interest
of self–esteem,
both yours
and what is left of mine,
I must ask you
to leave the room
before my behavior
smacks your person.

HIS DREADFUL CAR

Scientists tell us
the most ubiquitous cockroach in the world
originated in Germany
and so did his VW bug, hatched in '69
and to this day not quite dead.
It drags its decaying little body
across the face of the earth
swilling oil
belching poison
and sucking on borrowed money
seventy–five dollars at a time.
I hate his dreadful car.

Someday he will go out to the driveway
and we will hear a cry of disbelief
when he finds
his dreadful car
with a wooden stake through its carburetor
and a head of garlic
attached to its intake manifold.

And I will say, I have no idea
who could have done
such a thing.
But it is clearly a case
of manifold destiny.

DO I EMBARRASS YOU, MY DEAR?

I have been made aware
that I sometimes embarrass you
by the way I laugh,
the way I sometimes hum a tune,
the way I look at you, or anyone,
or anything,
the way I dress, comb my hair,
walk, sit, stand, smile,
or don't smile;
and by the way, on occasion,
I breathe funny.

I embarrass you, who at five
was taken to lunch at my aunt's house
and announced, "Oh goodie, we get napkins!
At home my mom just walks around the table
with a sponge."

I embarrass you, who at ten
after an hour in line at Great America
said to the lady in front of us,
"Oh, I love those socks of yours with the
big pink fuzzy balls on the backs,
but my mom won't let me get them
because she says they look so tacky."
And we had to stand there behind that lady
for another half hour.

I embarrass you, who at fifteen
sat across from me in the crowded Chinese restaurant
and said, in that piercing voice,
"Mom, I hope you don't take hormones
now that you're, you know,
near meniopause or whatever it is,
because in my Sex Ed class the teacher said
if you don't be careful with that stuff
you could get hair on your nipples."
There may never again be a moment
so silent
in that Chinese restaurant.

Do I embarrass you, my dear?
Well, I would like to say
something about that.

Hallelujah.

ALL I AM ASKING

Look, all I am asking is to borrow your car
for one lousy day at the beach.
You know perfectly well that my so–called car
gets lousy mileage and has no tapedeck
and is a piece of garbage.
Now I suppose I have to hear about how
you never had a car and
took the bus to the prom or something.

     Forget it, Rob.

Look, all I am asking
is for one happy day
listening to my music,
being with my friends,
driving a decent car
for a change and—

     For a change let John drive.

John can't drive—no he *can't*,
he has to take his mother to the hospital.
No, she's not sick, she's having amniocentesis.

     What are you telling me? As in *pregnant*?

Yeah. I guess they have to find out
if it's a retard or something because she's old.

She is forty–five and has
John with the waxed eight–inch crewcut and
Valerie with the "Let's Get It On" t–shirt
and Vishnu—I can't even look at Vishnu—
and she's *pregnant*?

Yeah. It's sort of weird. Well, hey,
can I borrow your car or not?

Take it.

Wow! Are you kidding? I mean, you know,
thanks a lot.

(Look, all I am asking,
at the least,
is not to be forty–five, pregnant,
and amniocentesed.)

ALASKA

Just give me one good reason,
he says,
why hitchhiking across Alaska is such a terrible idea,
when the whole plan has been explained to you,
and I have thought of everything,
just give me one good reason.
See? You can't! You can't think of a thing to say
except "No." Your big word.
Boy, you just can't stand to face the fact that
your kids don't need you to tie their shoelaces anymore.
No way, man, not you.

      Well, Ben, I guess I just, uh,
      feel uncomfortable with the Alaska idea
      but it's, uh, hard to put into words...
      (Because you'll end up living on wild turnips and Ho–Ho's
      after you lose your wallet like that time in the
      Pine Barrens. Or camping on a beach and being overwhelmed
      at 4 a.m. by enraged walruses
      protecting their mating grounds, and every night
      as I fall asleep I will see you getting beaten up
      by Eskimos with drinking problems
      or leaving your jacket somewhere
      and coming down with hypothermia
      or getting frostbite out in the tundra from wearing
      those tennis shoes with the holes in them
      and having your toes amputated by a midwife
      who is the only available medical person.
      And, as it so happens,
      both of your shoes are untied right this minute.)

Mom, I have never wanted to do anything
as much as I want to hitchhike through Alaska.
But you can't see it, can you?
Not you.
Sometimes I wonder
what you would be like
if you had an imagination.

SMOKING

I cannot believe
that after all those years
when I was smoking,
and you hated it,
the years when you left
notes on the refrigerator:

      DON'T DIE MOM QUIT NOW

The years you hung out the car window
with those theatrical
consumptive coughs

      (That's all right, Mom.
      Never mind if your kids
      get emphysema)

The years when I would look in my purse
for my cigarettes
and find them
mashed up into a little ball—

It is beyond belief
that today
I walk into your room
and you have left for school
but the memory of your Marlboros
lingers on.

WEED

Hey, aren't you home a little late?
Oh my God, look at those eyes.
Don't even try with the allergy bit,
because even my stupidity
has its limits
and the goldenrod's
been dead for a month.

We will not have this, do you understand?
This is out, boy, this is really out.
Oh good, stand there with that smile—
so warm, so communicative—
so stoned.
If your pupils
were any more dilated
your eyesockets
could give birth to your brain,
such as it is.

And don't waste what's left of your breath
telling me about people who drink Martinis
and run people over
because I drink Oolong tea and Diet Slice
and I haven't run anyone over
yet.

And to think my parents griped
about raising teenagers. Boy oh boy.
When I was sixteen, my father found
two lousy Winstons and an
airplane miniature bourbon bottle
rolled up in a sweatsock in my underwear drawer
and threatened to personally drive me
to the Milwaukee County Reform School
for Incorrigible Female Adolescents,
which for twenty-five years
I believed existed.
But this, this is my real punishment:
Life on the vice squad.
Life scared out of my wits that
something will happen,
that before you are old enough to know better
you will lose the chance
to be old enough to know better.

Oh, go to bed. Just go to bed.
I'd rather talk about it in the morning anyway,
after I've had time.
I need time.
Time for what, I don't know.

I was fairly stupid myself at sixteen,
but there was so much less
to be stupid about in 1957.
And stupidity, like everything else,
was much less expensive
in 1957.

Time for what, I don't know.

AT MCDONALDS, THEN AND NOW

It was a famous fight.
Sharon was fourteen and Margaret was ten
and they were supposed to be holding down a table
while the Mom stood in line
and what the fight was about the Mom never knew.
All she knew was that Margaret was suddenly beside her
bawling and yelling and Sharon was at the table,
thunder–faced, and a lady walked up and said,
"I don't like to interfere but
I saw that big one
hit the little one right in the face, hard."

The kind of moment in which one thinks,
right now other women are running famous restaurants,
or in the Boston Marathon, or for Congress,
and this is my life,
standing in line at McDonalds
while the big one hits the little one
right in the face, hard.

And now, Sharon is eighteen
and it's Saturday and she's working
the eleven to four shift at McDonalds.
I am standing in line, to surprise her
(Will she hate this? She'll hate this—
I'm leaving—)
But it's too late,
she looks up, amazed,
and she says,
"Omigosh, it's my *mom!*"
and a huge smile lights up her face.
See, the important thing is,
the first thing that happened
when she saw me
was the smile.

The kind of moment in which one thinks
right now
this is my life, standing in line at McDonalds,
and I am so grateful.

I LIKE YOU BETTER NOW

Babies smile back
every time you smile at them.
And babies never wish
that you were someone else, and so were they.
And babies, even when they're
hungry, dirty, or sick
never think that it is your fault.
And what is more, after you have got them
full, clean, or feeling better,
babies look downright grateful.

Yet, when I think of you
at seven months
crying all night from mal de tooth
if you want to know the honest truth,
I like you better now.
And when I think of you
at terrible two
(and three, and four)
kicking on the K–Mart floor
I like you better now.

Through the thick and thin of adolescence
it's not all sulks and alienation.
Sometimes there's even—*conversation!*

I like you better now.

Life After High School

INDEPENDENCE

Hello. This is your mother.
I just went to the bank
to put a deposit in our so–called joint account
and I am livid. *Livid.*
You call the way you are living "independence"?
There you were on the video screen with your
two dollar and three cent balance.
I'd have known you anywhere.
But that was nothing.
How could you possibly get
seven overdraft charges—ten bucks times seven
asinine stupid bounced checks—seventy bucks!
and on top of everything
look at the checks—
Four dollars and fifty nine cents for this,
seven dollars and forty five cents for that—
What the hell is the matter with you?
I give up. I just give up.

Why didn't you just throw seventy bucks
down the toilet? Just wad it up and
stand there and flush it down.

Well?

            Are you through screaming at me?

You think that was screaming?
I'll show you screaming.
I am full of screams.
I drove home from the bank screaming
with all the windows up
and I still have plenty left.

Let me tell you
what independence does not mean:
It does not mean
going away from home
to drink beer and get laid and go to parties and
live in a pigsty with a 1.8 GPA.
Independence means making your bed once in awhile
and picking your clothes up off the floor
and balancing your goddam checkbook.

       And I suppose that's what you thought
       when you were nineteen.

Certainly.

IF ONLY YOU

If only you
had encouraged me to go out for soccer
instead of buying me art junk
If only you
had encouraged my art
instead of shoving me onto a soccer field
If only you
had cared enough to take some action
when I got D's in algebra and chemistry
If only you
had cared about something besides grades
instead of nagging me about a couple of lousy D's
If only you
had had the guts to set some limits
when I discovered booze and pot
If only you
had not freaked out just because
I did a little booze and pot
If only you
had even considered me capable of a spiritual side
and talked about religion, much less God
If only you
had not jammed your religion down my throat
and turned me off that stuff completely
If only you
had not smothered and overprotected me
as if I were a giant baby until I was twenty
If only you
had not expected me to figure everything out myself
before I was old enough to know right from wrong

I wonder what I might have been by now.

THANKSGIVING I: The Invitation

Ring ring ring, "I have a collect call
from Rob—
will you accept the charge?"
Hey, Mom, how're you doin'? Hey, that's great.
Sure looking forward to Thanksgiving.
I was sort of wondering
whether it would be OK with you guys
if a couple of friends of mine
had Thanksgiving dinner with us.
Hey, that's great.
Actually, three friends.
Hey, that's very generous of you.
Wait a minute, somebody's talking to me.
(HEY SHUT UP YOU GUYS SHUT UP SHUT UP
SHE JUST INVITED YOU FOR THANKSGIVING)
Mom, you still there?
Yeah, Dan wants to know
should they bring sleeping bags
or do we have enough beds?
Well, I figured Dan and Deirdre
could sleep in Margaret's bed, and—
what?
OK, they'll bring the bags.
One other thing.
We're all, like, ovolactovegetarians.
Hey, it's no prob.

More bird for you guys, right?

THANKSGIVING II: The Arrival

Three friends have been brought
home for Thanksgiving
and the parents are not sure
whether to set three more places
or dial 911.

The mother is telling herself
that appearance is not what counts. And yet.

Debbie is wearing
periwinkle blue bangs
and a hair ornament
that resembles an office supply.

Deirdre is wearing
Marcel Marceau make–up and a black cowl,
and looks like she should be
modeling for highway safety posters,
carrying a scythe.

Daniel is wearing one earring
and a pair of shorts, that's it,
with a skateboard slung over one shoulder.

Debbie with the blue bangs,
it turns out,
is majoring in biochemistry.
Marcel Marceau is an art history graduate student.
Daniel is majoring in Peace.

All right, so they're nice kids,
the Father says to the Mother, later,
but do they have to look so—
unattractive?

What matters,
says the Mother,
to the propagation of the species,
is not that they attract you
but that they attract
each other.

But,
says the Father,
is this the species
we want propagated?

55

THANKSGIVING III: The Morning After

I don't care how perfectly natural our bodies are
or how much they look alike—
which notion, as a matter of fact,
is trashola to the twelfth power—
you and your friends
are *not* going to walk around this house stark naked.
My God, Rob, have you lost your *mind*?
Your little sister Margaret is in this house
not to mention your father who is in such a rage
that he has had to go to Hardware Universe
to walk around and get calmed down.

And how dare you say that I
have no concept of the free body when one year ago
anybody who accidentally walked into your room
when your body happened to be free
was taking their life in their hands—
and now I should put up with you and Dan
microwaving mashed potatoes in the buff?
And believe me, if I live to be a hundred
I won't forget
that rear view of Deirdre and Debbie
scrambling eggs.
What if Grandma had stopped by for coffee?
No. No. Why torture myself.

For this you went to college?

       Do you want an honest answer to that question, Mom?

No.

THE EMPTY NEST

And so she was off, the last of the kids to go,
with all her cardboard boxes
crammed into the aging Datsun.

The mom and dad waved and waved as she drove away,
and then they shut the door, and turned back
into the empty nest.
And when they shut the door, there was
no
sound.

They found that unless they messed it up themselves
the house looked pretty good most of the time.
The dad bought a bag of miniature Snickers
to savor gradually
and after three days there were still a couple left.
The mom walked around in a new leotard and tights
and went to an aerobics class with some other women
whose daughters had also moved away
taking their thirty–two inch hips with them
and the moms jumped up and down to Lionel Ritchie tapes
and knew that they were getting better, not older.

The mom and dad discovered
listening to music in the evening
the leisurely reading of newspapers in the morning
and romance in the afternoon.

One day, the last of the kids to go
called long distance and said,
It must seem sort of weird around there,
like, just the two of you.
Well, said the mom,
It is different.
And the daughter said, Well, hang in there.
You'll get used to it.

And the dad said, You bet.

HOME FOR THE SUMMER

Somehow there had been an idea
that he would get a job on a field team
south of here,
and she would get a job as a camp counselor,
north of here,
but now it is June, and the two of them
are home for the summer.

The boy says, "I'm welcome, aren't I?"
and the father replies,
"Welcome? What a question.
Isn't this your home?
Aren't I your father?"
And the father takes another sip of his coffee
from a cup that he has never drunk out of
because the boy
is drinking his coffee
from the father's blue mug.

The girl says, "You don't mind having me here, do you?"
and the mother says,
"Mind? Why should I mind?
Aren't I your mother?
Isn't this your home?"
And the mother goes to the freezer
for her Weight Watcher's Sausage Pizza,
but it is gone.

The next morning, the parents go out for lunch
and when they return at 1:25 p.m.,
the boy and girl have just got up,
because they had a late night.
They are eating breakfast and
reading the newspaper. He is wearing
his roommate's bathrobe, the one with
the bleach spots; she is wearing long underwear,
mukluks and a poncho. The father thinks,
They could be a pair of economic refugees
waiting to be placed.

And the boy says,
"Hey, next time you guys buy eggs,
how about getting jumbos?"

Isn't the dad their dad?
Isn't the mom their mom?

Isn't this their home?

DANCIN' IN THE STREETS

The mom is being taken, as a Mother's Day present
to the Grateful Dead concert
which she rightfully interprets
as a tender compliment.
The Grateful Dead concert is
way, way, way up in some hills above Monterey, California,
and they walk in the blinding sun
straight up for two miles, with 20,000 people,
and the kids tell her,
Now remember, Mom, if anyone offers you anything
to eat or drink, like strawberries, for example...
Yes, I'll remember, she says. I'll tell them,
"My kids don't let me eat between meals,
but thanks anyway,"
and the mom finally comes to terms
with the fact that the great role reversal has begun
which she had begun to suspect that morning
because until today she drove the car
because she was the mom, but today
the son drove the car
because he was the man.
And way, way, way up in the hills
somewhere above Monterey, California,
they dance and dance and dance,
and she remembers
when she danced to the Doors in 1968
and she tells them, Hey, I danced to the Doors
in 1968, when you guys were home,
sucking on a zwieback and
practicing your projectile vomiting.

The indulgent smiles on their faces
make her feel like one of the geezers
who shows up every year to celebrate
the Great San Francisco Earthquake of '06,
the survivors.
But oh, how she had danced, that night in '68,
in that red velvet mini–dress
that might even still fit,
as an oven mitt.
And oh, how she dances today,
and feels that she could dance
forever through those hills where the sky is as blue,
the sun as yellow, the clouds as white, and the grass as green
as in the pictures they brought home from kindergarten.
They clap, and they sing, with the other 20,000 people,
"Our lo—o—o—ve
will not fa—a—ade
a—wa—a—ay..."
two hundred times, at the tops of their voices,
and she thinks, Oh my dears, my dears...
ain't it the truth.